experiencing GOD

40 meditations to connect with God in daily life

SHIREEN CHADA

978-1-941883-20-4 (Paperback)
978-1-941883-17-4 (Ebook)

Published in the United States of America.

Cover Design: Michael Mackintosh

For permissions or inquiries, please contact: releaseyourwings@gmail.com

To BapDada:

my Teacher, my Friend, my Beloved.

Books and Meditation Albums
by Shireen Chada

Books

Experiencing God

Awakening from the Matrix

The Trust Revolution

God's Blessings for You

Soul Fitness

Oh My Goodness!

Insperience the Divine

Meditation Albums

The Eight Spiritual Powers

Real Reflections

The Sweet Melody of Silence

Connect with Shireen Chada

I would love to stay connected with you on your journey.

Listen to Shireen's latest podcast episodes on ***Spiritual Sense***, available wherever you get your podcasts.

For current meditations, free resources, and audio courses, visit: releaseyourwings.org

TABLE OF CONTENTS

A NOTE FOR YOU

This is not a treatise; it is a lived remembrance. I use the word God and the pronoun He on purpose. I am speaking about the One, not a vague "divine energy," but the living Being I have come to know: the Ocean of Love, the single Source from whom every pure feeling of love arises.

"He" is my devotional shorthand, the language of relationship, not a claim about gender. The One is beyond gender. Throughout these chapters you will also meet God as Mother, Friend, Teacher, and Child. If another name opens your heart more easily, use it. The Love is One.

This work is intentionally simple and unvarnished. In my other books I worked with editors to polish every page. Here I kept the edits few so the voice would stay close to the heart. What you will see is meditation of the heart turned into practice.

This book is uniform by design. Each chapter follows the same two-part structure to create a steady rhythm for daily practice.

How to Engage

This is a dip-in journey. Each chapter stands alone.

- **The Sacred Reality** offers a clear window into an aspect of God.
- **In My Heart** turns that truth into intimate remembrance, a short, first-person meditation.

A Simple Way to Use This Book

1. Pause. Sit comfortably and let the breath settle.
2. Open or select any chapter. Take **The Sacred Reality** slowly.
3. Turn to **In My Heart**. Read it slowly, as if already true. Adjust any name for God so it lands naturally.
4. Carry one line. Choose a sentence from anywhere in the chapter as your gentle focus for the day.

Read slowly, letting the silences speak. When you feel a natural pause, rest there in remembrance before moving on.

May these offerings help you not just think about God, but meet God, in living meditation, again and again, until knowing travels from mind to heart.

1

The Point of Light

God is not a vast form or
a majestic figure carved in stone.
He is a Point of living Light.

The Sacred Reality

Across history, humanity has tried to capture God in images, temples, and rituals. We have built towering memorials to hold this divine presence. Yet the truth is simpler, and more wondrous: God is a radiant Point of Light, beyond shadow.

Just as the seed of a tree holds within it the future of branches, leaves, and fruit, so this infinitesimal Point contains all wisdom, all love, all power.

He is subtle beyond sight, yet nothing greater exists. In a world obsessed with grandeur, divine greatness hides in simplicity. The Infinite appears as a Point. The Highest on High remains unseen by bodily eyes, yet dazzles the eye of the soul. Nearer than thought and wider than every horizon, He is neither diffused into matter nor contained by it.

To see God as a Point of Light is to see ourselves reflected, for we, too, are points of living light. The child resembles the Parent. When we remember God in this form, we remember who we truly are.

In My Heart ♥

When I first learned that God is a Point of Light, not a figure of myth or imagination, it was as though a veil lifted. Suddenly God was no longer far away or unreachable. He was nearer than breath: simple, pure, personal.

I carry the Point like a quiet compass; my steps begin to align.

This awareness stripped away the weight of superstition and brought me into a relationship of clarity. I needed only a shift in vision, to see through the eye of the soul. When I glimpse that tiny flame shining in the silence of eternity, I know I am home with Him.

In God's light,
I discover my own brilliance.

Write your reflections here . . .

2

The Incorporeal One (*Nirakari*)

God has no body, no outline,
no image to contain divine Being.
He is the Incorporeal One,
Nirakari, beyond matter itself.

The Sacred Reality

Every human being is tied to a form. We see, speak, and act through the body. Even the noblest saints are remembered by their appearance. But God alone remains forever bodiless, not flesh or bone, not confined by space or time. In a world of forms, God is rare here, not absent, but never diffused into matter, never contained by it.

As incorporeal, He abides in the eternal Home of silence and light, beyond this physical universe, beyond the cycle of birth and death. No sculpture can capture this essence; no temple can hold such presence. God is the subtlest reality: pure conscious Light. Because He is beyond the elements, He is never stained by them. God is known by remembrance, not by the senses.

Here's the paradox: though formless, He is not abstract, not a faceless void, nor an impersonal energy. He is living, personal, knowable, the Parent of all souls. When it is time to serve, He acts without taking birth, speaking through a chosen chariot, giving inheritance, then returning to His incorporeal Home.

In My Heart ♥

When I remember God as *Nirakari*, my vision shifts. I stop searching for Him in images or rituals and meet Him in awareness. I turn inward to who I am, the soul, and upward to the Bodiless One. This divine formlessness makes Him more intimate, not less.

This experience lightens me. In His presence, the masks of body and role fall away. I am no longer cramped by labels or appearances; I rest as a soul, embraced by the Luminous Light.

In God's bodiless presence,
the soul becomes
weightless and free.

Write your reflections here . . .

3

Beyond Birth and Death (*Ajanma*)

All souls are born, live, and die within the cycle of time. But God is *Ajanma*, the One who is never born, never dies, never bound by birth and death.

The Sacred Reality

Every being in creation takes birth in a body. Even the highest souls descend and ascend, playing their part upon the stage of the world. Birth brings limitation; death brings change. But God alone remains outside this cycle.

Because He is never born, He never forgets; because He never dies, He never fears. His existence is constant, beyond decay, beyond time. While all others are actors, He is the eternal Witness and Director, entering the stage only to guide, never to become trapped in the play.

Here, the wonder is this: He serves the world of birth and death without ever becoming subject to it. God comes to serve, yet does not take birth. He works through a chosen instrument, yet does not claim a body as His own. He acts through another, yet remains beyond action. The One is free, utterly, eternally.

In My Heart ♥

When I reflect on God as *Ajanma*, the grip of mortality loosens. Death no longer feels like an end but a doorway. If the One is beyond birth and death, then I too, as a soul, am beyond. My part may change, my costumes may change, yet my essence is indestructible.

This realization restores courage. I do not cling to the temporary as if it were forever. Instead, I draw strength from the One who is forever. To know Him as *Ajanma* is to remember that the soul is ageless, timeless, deathless.

I see endings as passages, not cliffs. I stop bargaining for more time and start using this moment cleanly.

In God's eternity,
the soul remembers
its own immortality.

Write your reflections here . . .

4

The Ocean of Knowledge

God is not a scholar or philosopher.
He is the Ocean of Knowledge,
the One who holds the secrets of time
and truth within His being.

The Sacred Reality

Human knowledge rises and falls with the ages. What one era calls wisdom, the next calls error. Even the greatest thinkers are bound by their time, but God alone sees the whole cycle from beginning to end; His sight encompasses origin and return.

When God speaks, it is not from accumulated wisdom but from perfect knowing, what has always been and will be again. This knowledge is not written in books; it lives in His being. Saints and sages touch a drop of truth; He is the Ocean. In Him there are no contradictions, no missing pieces, no borrowed thoughts.

Here is the wonder: the Highest on High speaks in the simplest words. He does not lecture like a philosopher; He explains as a Father to children, plain, precise, nourishing.

In My Heart ♥

When I first began to listen, I realized God's words carried a lightness unlike human teaching. There was no pride, no demand, only clarity. The fog of confusion lifted, and life began to feel like a story I finally understood.

For me, this divine knowledge is not heavy with rules but filled with freedom. It tells me who I am, why I am here, and where I am going. Each time I listen, I taste a drop from the Ocean, and that drop is enough to guide a day.

In His company, I stop skimming the shore of ideas and go inward, deeper. I turn one point quietly until it yields strength. I do not chase novelty; I return to the same truth until it imprints.

In God's knowledge, confusion dissolves and truth becomes simple.

Write your reflections here . . .

5

The Ever Pure One

God is so deeply involved in our upliftment,
yet so completely detached,
and this is the secret
of His eternal purity.

The Sacred Reality

Human beings stumble through the cycle of falling and rising. Time has clouded all of us, but never God. His purity is not something He earns, recovers, or defends; it simply is. He is the light that never gathers smoke.

For us, purity often feels fragile, a vow to keep, an effort to resist waste. For Him, purity is effortless. Where ours falters and fluctuates, He remains steady in eternity.

Here is the paradox: He enters the dirtiest age, yet not a speck of dust clings to Him. Only the One who has never lost purity can awaken it again in others.

This is why His purity is power. What trembles in us under pressure is unshakable in Him. He enters the impure world so that even the most stained can remember their own innocence.

In My Heart ♥

Knowing God as the Ever Pure One has changed how I see purity itself. In His company, I discover that purity is not austerity; it is joy, cheerfulness, and power. When I am near Him, purity feels like prosperity, the prosperity of being embraced by a love so complete that vice loses its hold.

In His purity, I remember that purity is my original nature, for as His child, I carry the same seed of truth. Mine, too, is not destroyed, only hidden beneath the weight of many lifetimes.

When impurity stirs within me, I do not have to resist it. I need only surrender it into His love, and it dissolves. In the light of His purity, I do not feel accused or condemned; I feel restored to the self I had forgotten.

In God's purity,
my heart learns
its own innocence.

Write your reflections here . . .

6

The Ocean of Love

God is the Ocean of Love:
steady, endless, and overflowing
toward every soul.

The Sacred Reality

Human love, though precious, is often mixed with need or expectation. It rises and falls with moods and circumstances, sometimes strong, sometimes weak. But God's love is different. It is pure; it does not cling, it does not demand, it does not tire.

God does not love me for my role, my actions, or my appearance. He loves because it is His nature to love. Like the sun that shines on mountain and valley alike, this divine love reaches every soul, saint or sinner, strong or weak. God gives without keeping account, without ever running dry.

Here is the wonder: this love is as vast as an ocean, yet it touches me as though I were the only one. In the expanse of eternity, He makes space for intimacy. This is the miracle of divine love, unlimited, yet deeply personal.

In My Heart ♥

When I experience His love, something softens inside me. The restless search for approval falls silent. I no longer need to be chosen or praised by the world, because I am already held by God.

This love lifts without binding, heals without possession. It shows me how to love others with the same open hand, not grasping, not keeping score, but freely giving. God's love fills the deepest thirst of my heart, the ancient longing of lifetimes.

To call Him the Ocean of Love is to admit that words fail. No measure can contain this presence; no vessel can hold such love. I can only return again and again, letting these waves wash over me until my heart learns to love as He loves.

In God's love,
I am already home.

Write your reflections here . . .

7

The Ocean of Peace

I am peace. The Home is peace.
The Father is the Ocean of Peace.
Our true religion is peace. This is not
a mood; it's a map: who I am,
where I belong, whom I belong to.
And how to live: in peace.

The Sacred Reality

Every soul longs for peace, yet many confuse it with escape: a quiet room, a mountain retreat, a pause from noise. But God's peace is not an interval between struggles; it is eternal, unbroken, beyond circumstance.

God is never pulled by sorrow, never shaken by storms. The world turns in turmoil, but this divine presence remains unmoved, like the silent depths beneath the ocean's waves.

We lose peace over the smallest matters: a word, a glance, an unexpected change. His stillness, however, is limitless. Nothing disturbs Him; nothing clings to His being. He abides in silence, beyond the reach of fear, loss, or desire. Peace is His nature, not a response to conditions.

Here is the divine paradox: though God is silence itself, He comes into the noisiest age to give that silence back to us. He does not silence the world; He awakens silence within the soul.

In My Heart ♥

When I remember God as the Ocean of Peace, my thoughts settle like dust in clear water. The urge to fix, defend, or chase loosens. Peace is not outside me; it flows from Him, through me, and into life.

This stillness does not pull me away; it anchors me at the center of activity. Peace is not weakness but strength, not emptiness but fullness. From this quiet center, I speak fewer words and choose kinder ones.

I lift my vision, soul to the Ocean of Peace. In this meeting, the heart remembers Home; peace becomes not an event but my atmosphere.

In God's stillness,
the soul remembers
its eternal strength.

Write your reflections here . . .

8

The Purifier

God is the Purifier, and I am the one being purified. This is the meeting: God's purity cleanses; my remembrance of Him receives.

The Sacred Reality

All other beings, no matter how elevated, become stained by time. Every soul gathers the dust of sorrow and the rust of forgetfulness. But God alone remains forever stainless, beyond the reach of karma or decay. From this divine purity comes the power to purify.

The world has searched for purity in rivers, fire, and ritual. Yet water can only wash the body, not the heart; fire can only burn what is seen, not what is hidden. God's purity alone reaches the soul, washing the deep impressions of sorrow, fear, and guilt that nothing else can touch.

Here is the divine paradox: the One who has never fallen comes to lift those who have. The One who never tasted impurity enters the impure world not to judge, but to heal. He cleanses without condemning, liberates without force, restores without reminding us of the stain.

In My Heart ❤

When I experience God as the Purifier, I stop fearing my past. The weight of mistakes no longer feels permanent. God's presence works like a gentle flame, burning what is false, revealing what is eternal in me.

This gives me courage to stand in dignity again, not because I am flawless, but because He is. His purity reminds me that the soul is not broken, only covered. In remembrance, those coverings loosen and fall.

I do not wrestle with the stain; I offer it. In God's light, guilt turns into learning, and the heart grows simple again.

In God's purity,
the soul shines again
as it was in the beginning.

Write your reflections here . . .

9

The Quiet One

God is not noisy. He does not
dazzle or gather admirers.
He waits in silence and prefers
the whisper of love to worship.

The Sacred Reality

When the world builds temples, God does not rush there. He is present in the stillness of a quiet heart. He prefers the company of one soul remembering Him over a thousand voices chanting names without awareness. His way is simple and hidden: He comes to serve, to teach, and then goes, without asking for garlands or recognition.

This is the divine personality: He does not like attention. God does not court followers, stage displays, or demand ritual applause. The Highest on High calls Himself the obedient Servant; the Ocean of Treasures arrives incognito, gives what is needed, and leaves no trace except peace.

Here is the paradox: the subtlest presence is the most powerful. God does not raise His voice to be heard; He quiets our noise so we can hear. He does not press on anyone; He makes space in us for truth to arise. In a world frantic to be seen, He heals by being unseen.

In My Heart ♥

Knowing God as the Quiet One has changed how I come to Him. I no longer try to attract His attention. I let the need for attention fall away. I sit in the steady pause, and in that gentleness His presence becomes unmistakable.

His quiet reshapes my living. I speak less and listen longer. I choose hidden service over display, and I leave outcomes to Him. When I am provoked, I choose the pause instead of the reply; what would have become a storm becomes a passage for peace.

Silence is no longer withdrawal; it is a door He opens within me. From that door, blessings pass through without my name attached.

In that quiet,
the heart learns
God's voice.

Write your reflections here . . .

10

The Most Free

God is the most free:
unbound by time, matter, or praise.
Because He belongs to none,
He can belong to all.

The Sacred Reality

Human beings cling: to possessions, to roles, to praise and blame, to the weight of the past and the worry of the future. Even while longing for freedom, we bind ourselves with expectation. But God is beyond all this. No role defines Him; no ritual confines Him.

God is not trapped in images or shrines. He comes when He chooses, as He chooses, and leaves quietly. Even while acting through a body, He is never caught by it. His nature is pure detachment, not coldness, but the liberty to give completely without needing to keep.

Here is the paradox: such freedom does not make God distant; it makes Him near to all. Because He is unbound, He can belong to everyone without partiality. Owning nothing, He can give everything.

In My Heart ♥

When I remember God as the most free, the knots in me begin to loosen. I see how often I hand myself to roles, reactions, and reputation. I stop bargaining for approval and set down the need to be understood. Freedom then is not license; it is the end of inner slavery.

In remembrance, soul to God, I practice open hands. I return what is not mine to carry: others' choices, yesterday's story, tomorrow's outcome. I do what is mine with love and leave the rest unclaimed. With that release, breathing eases; the soul sheds its armor; I move without chains.

God's freedom becomes my pattern: duty without bondage, love without claim, service without ownership, speech without the urge to convince. When fear tightens, I step back to the quiet center and say, "I place this in Your care." The knot weakens; the path widens.

In God's freedom,
the soul learns
to fly again.

Write your reflections here . . .

11

The Humble Giver

God is the Highest on High,
yet He comes as a servant.
He gives everything and
keeps nothing for Himself.

The Sacred Reality

Human generosity often carries a shadow: a wish to be seen, thanked, remembered. God's giving is different. He arrives quietly, brings what is needed, and leaves no trace except peace. He does not gather admirers or collect offerings. God calls Himself the Obedient Servant, not because He is less, but because love makes Him willing to serve all, without preference or parade.

Here is the wonder: the Sovereign refuses a throne; the Ocean pours Himself into a single thirsty heart. He teaches without display, uplifts without announcement, and vanishes into silence when the work is done.

His humility is not shyness; it is majesty without need. Because He is full, He does not seek; because He is complete, He does not take. His joy is to bestow: wisdom for the lost, strength for the weary, love for the wounded, dignity for the forgotten.

In My Heart ♥

Meeting Him as the Humble Giver changes how I serve. I notice where I still want credit, where I reach for praise or proof that I matter. His example loosens those cravings. I begin to give because giving is beautiful, not because it is noticed. I learn to step in when needed and step back when done, leaving blessings, not signatures.

God does not bargain, measure, or keep accounts. The little I offer, one honest thought, one clean intention, He multiplies into fortunes.

When I remember Him, I feel a quiet abundance flow through me. What I share is not mine; it is His, passing through. And that is freedom.

From God's open hand,
my heart learns to give
without needing to be seen.

Write your reflections here . . .

12

The Comforter of Hearts (*Dilaram*)

God is not only the Almighty.
He is *Dilaram*, the Comforter of Hearts,
the One who eases sorrow with
His presence.

The Sacred Reality

Human comfort, though sincere, is often fragile. People may say kind words, but their own hearts carry pain. They may listen, but they cannot take away the weight. God alone comforts without demand, without fatigue. His nearness cools the burning mind, soothes the restless heart, and restores hope where despair had settled.

He is pleased not by cleverness but by honesty of heart. A soul that comes to God, simple and true, receives solace instantly. He asks for no offerings, no elaborate prayers, only an open heart. This is His paradox: the Highest of all is moved not by power or status, but by sincerity.

To those who grieve, God is rest. To those who are weary, He is relief. God does not erase difficulties, but He steadies the soul to walk through them without breaking. His comfort is quiet, steady, unshakable.

In My Heart ♥

When I come to God in sorrow, His comfort feels more real than words. He may not change the outer scene, but He changes me: the breath deepens, the chest unclenches, the mind stops circling. What felt like a cliff becomes a path.

In remembrance, soul to God, I rest awhile in His quiet. A coolness spreads through the heat of worry; a simple courage returns. The burden does not vanish, yet I no longer carry it alone. I place it in His keeping, and I walk lighter.

He shows me that comfort is strength: the power to endure with dignity, to heal without hardening, to stand up again without bitterness. Remembering Him as *Dilaram*, I learn to comfort as He does: presence before answers, love before advice, listening before speech.

In God's comfort,
my heart learns
to rest without fear.

Write your reflections here . . .

13

The Silent Companion

God does not follow us noisily through life. He accompanies in silence, present the instant a heart remembers.

The Sacred Reality

Human companions often comfort by talking, advising, or filling space. God comforts by presence. He does not intrude, persuade, or demand attention. God waits, unobtrusive, patient, until a soul turns inward and upward. Then His nearness is unmistakable: a settling of the mind, a softening of the breath, a strength that does not announce itself.

God's companionship does not crowd; it creates room. In truth, He does not "remember" as we do, holding on and worrying. The Companion remains free, and because He is free, He can be flawlessly faithful.

This is the divine paradox: the One who never binds is the safest company; the One who never insists is the most constant support. God comes without footsteps and leaves without absence, the Friend who stands beside you without standing in your way.

In My Heart ♥

When I walk into uncertainty, I remember Him and feel the ground under my feet. Fear loosens its grip. I do not need signs or voices; His companionship arrives as clarity and calm courage.

In the small pauses of the day, I find Him waiting: the quiet moment before sleep, the first breath upon waking. His companionship teaches me that presence matters more than words, that listening creates more space than talking.

When loneliness visits, that hollow ache that no amount of company seems to fill, I turn to the silent Companion and discover I was never truly alone. He doesn't crowd the emptiness with noise or distraction; instead, He fills it with a presence so real that solitude transforms from punishment into sanctuary. In His quiet company, I learn that being alone and being lonely are entirely different countries.

In God's quiet company,
my steps become steady
and my heart unafraid.

Write your reflections here . . .

14

The Innocent Lord

God is Lord of all, yet utterly
innocent: the One who gives
without keeping accounts
and trusts without hesitation.

The Sacred Reality

In the world, cleverness is praised. People guard themselves, measure what they give, and keep accounts of what they receive. But God is different. He keeps no ledger of merit or demerit; He does not weigh our offerings against our flaws. With a single drop of honest remembrance, He pours an ocean of blessings in return.

This is why God is called the Innocent Lord. His innocence is not ignorance; it is purity of heart. He sees the essence, not the fault. God looks past weakness to the spark of sincerity and is instantly pleased.

The paradox is this: the Highest of all is also the simplest of all. While human lords demand tribute, He accepts a true heart and gives a kingdom in exchange.

In My Heart ♥

His innocence disarms my fear. He does not come to accuse, calculate, or punish; God comes only to give, to uplift, to restore.

When I come in simple love, God places everything into my hands: strength, dignity, authority of spirit. Sometimes I want to pull back, to say "enough," fearing I cannot carry it well. Yet His innocence keeps pouring; God does not suspect or ration. He trusts me into who I am meant to become.

In remembrance, soul to God, I receive without flinching and ask for a clean heart to hold what He gives. Receiving becomes responsibility: not for display but for service, light to be shared, power to uplift, love to steady other hearts. I ask to spend what He entrusts the way He would: quietly, generously, without keeping score.

From God's innocent trust,
my heart learns to receive fully
and to serve wisely.

Write your reflections here . . .

15

The Friend (*Khuda Dost*)

God is the Almighty, yet
He chooses to be known as *Khuda Dost*,
the true Friend of every heart.

The Sacred Reality

Human friendships, though precious, are fragile. They can change with distance, with time, or with misunderstanding. Even the best of friends cannot always stay. But God is the Friend who never leaves, never grows tired, never turns away.

The Friend knows our weaknesses, yet He does not withdraw. God listens without judgment, accepts without demand. His friendship is not based on what we do but on who we are: souls, His children. He delights in our goodness even when we fail to see it. With God there is no need to impress, no need to hide.

Here is His paradox: the Highest on High, the One beyond birth and death, chooses to walk with us as a companion. God could remain far, untouched, unknown. Yet He draws near, saying simply and intimately, "You are Mine." His friendship is not lofty or formal; it is personal, warm, and constant.

In My Heart ❤

When I experience Him as my Friend, formality falls away. I can speak to God openly, sharing what is deepest in me without fear. At times I sense His nearness so strongly that it feels as though He is quietly enjoying my company, not because I am flawless, but because I belong to Him.

This friendship changes how I walk through life. With God beside me, the path feels lighter. With Him, I find the courage to stand steady, to be patient, to see others as friends rather than threats. His loyalty teaches me to stay when leaving would be easier, to be present without demand, to keep confidences and keep faith.

In God's friendship,
my heart learns
constancy and trust.

Write your reflections here . . .

16

The Traveler

God is not far away in His own world while
we struggle in this one.
He is the Traveler's Companion,
the One who walks with us on
the long road of life.

The Sacred Reality

Every soul is a traveler. We move through births and deaths, through changing roles and shifting scenes. Companions come and go; God is the Companion who never departs.

He does not remove the hills; He gives strength for the climb. God does not always shorten the miles; He makes the way sweet. A quiet gladness rises where He walks: shade in heat, a star at night, a cup of water when the mile feels long.

Here is His paradox: the Highest on High is also the humblest Companion. He holds the map of eternity, yet He adjusts His pace to ours. He knows the destination, yet stays close while we find the courage to continue.

In My Heart ♥

When I remember God as the Traveler beside me, the road straightens inside. I lift my vision, soul to God, and feel a steady pace set. He is patient yet firm: He meets me with love and calls me onward.

I begin to travel differently. I hand Him what I cannot carry: my sack of "why" and "how," the stones of regret and worry. In return, I find a staff of clarity in my hand and a lamp of peace at my feet. The path is still the path, but I am lighter and happier.

With Him, I choose the next right step instead of demanding the whole route. I look up more often, notice the sky, say thank you for small mileposts. When old fears rise at a bend, I pause in remembrance until courage returns, and then I walk on.

In God's company,
the journey grows light
and the heart glad.

Write your reflections here . . .

17

The Gentle Liberator

God does not conquer with fear or bind with rules. He is the Gentle Liberator, the One who sets souls free with compassion and love.

The Sacred Reality

The soul becomes trapped, bound by habits, by sorrow, by the weight of vices. We try to break free, yet in struggling we often tighten the chains. Human authority seeks to control through punishment, but God's way is different. He liberates without force, without humiliation.

He does not come to accuse but to release. God's purity weakens the grip of impurity. His compassion unties the knots of fear. By reminding us who we are, eternal, pure souls, God restores the freedom we thought was lost. This is why He is called the Liberator, the Compassionate One. Even the most fallen can rise through His compassion.

Here lies His paradox: the Almighty does not dominate. God's power is purity; His method, remembrance; His result, freedom. God grants liberation in life, not only at death. To be near Him is to feel lighter, more yourself, unbound from what once ruled you.

In My Heart ♥

When I remember Him as the Gentle Liberator, the tightness inside begins to ease. Worries lose their grip, habits loosen, and sorrow feels less permanent. God does not push me to change; He inspires me to want freedom.

Then joy slips in. Ordinary moments brighten: a quiet smile appears; a little current of love runs inside. Gratitude bubbles up. I catch myself humming; simple things feel enough. It is as if a small lamp is lit at the center, and the soul keeps a soft song in the background.

I learn that liberation is not escape from life but the strength to live it without chains.

In God's compassion,
my heart learns
that true power is freedom.

Write your reflections here . . .

18

The Hidden One

God works in silence, unseen,
asking for no recognition.
He is the Hidden One, who comes quietly,
serves fully, and returns without fanfare.

The Sacred Reality

The world celebrates what is loud and visible. Achievements are announced, names remembered, credit claimed. But God's way is different. He carries out the greatest task in history, purifying the world and granting liberation, and yet most do not recognize Him. He does it off-camera.

God chooses an ordinary body, speaks in ordinary words, and works in the most extraordinary way. His service is incognito, hidden from the eyes of the world. This is His paradox: the Highest of all does the highest work while remaining unseen. The One who could demand every garland prefers to stay unknown, reaching only the hearts that are searching.

His hiddenness is not weakness but humility. It protects God's work, for only those who truly seek will recognize Him. God asks for nothing, no worship, no attention, only remembrance. Not because He needs it, but because in His hidden way He gives without asking in return.

In My Heart ♥

When I remember Him as the Hidden One, I feel a pull toward simplicity. I do not need to announce what I do or seek appreciation. I see that the deepest service often happens quietly, without name or recognition.

In remembrance, I do the next right thing and let it go. I learn to sow and walk on, trusting that God tends the seed in ways I cannot see.

Joy grows in this way of living. I find sweetness in small acts of obedience, courage in quiet honesty, freedom in letting praise pass by. The heart feels light when it is not performing. I sense that He is building a morning and that my hidden yes is part of it.

In God's hiddenness,
my heart serves unseen
and trusts the dawn.

Write your reflections here . . .

19

The Patient One

The Almighty could command
instant obedience.
Instead, He chooses to wait.

The Sacred Reality

Human patience runs thin. We tire of waiting; we grow frustrated when others do not change on our schedule. We check our watches, tap our feet, lose faith. But God's patience is different; it is not endurance but love itself. This is the divine paradox: unlimited power expressed as unlimited patience.

He never forces, never compels. God waits. Even when we forget Him for lifetimes, He continues to hold the door open. Even when we resist His call, turn our backs, make the same mistakes again, He does not withdraw.

His patience is not passive but powerful: steady love that trusts the deeper timing of the heart. It is the confidence that no soul is beyond hope, that every prodigal will eventually turn Home.

In My Heart ♥

When I experience Him as the Patient One, the fear of failing softens. I stop rushing to prove myself worthy. He lets me grow at my own pace, and my steps find an honest, steady rhythm.

His patience shows me how to wait for others with the same faith. When someone I love is struggling, I learn to trust their process instead of trying to rush their healing. I stop checking the clock so often. I let conversations unfold without rushing to conclusions.

In my hardest seasons, I hear His gentle voice: "Have patience, O mind, your days of happiness are about to come." These words shift something inside. I stop demanding immediate relief and start trusting the arc of His love.

Then joy shows up quietly in this space: the day feels roomy; I can wait without fidgeting. I do the thing in front of me with a light hand and let the rest arrive in its time.

In God's patience,
my heart learns
to trust the timing of love.

Write your reflections here . . .

20

The Divine Mother

The Almighty veils His power in motherliness: belonging that steadies us, tenderness that teaches us to walk.

The Sacred Reality

Every soul carries a deep need to belong. Human mothers, though full of love, cannot give belonging that lasts forever. Their care is limited by time, fatigue, or circumstance. But God's motherly love is infinite. As the Divine Mother, He offers the embrace every soul longs for: complete, tireless, and secure.

This is His paradox: the Supreme, unlimited in power, expresses Himself in the most tender of ways. God does not see us through the eyes of failure or weakness; He sees us as beautiful, innocent, and whole. God's embrace is not only comfort but also courage. In that embrace, the soul remembers its worth, regains its strength, and begins to heal.

To belong to Him as Mother is to find a relationship that never ends. When human ties fade, His love remains. When the world overlooks us, He still holds us close. His care is strong enough to correct, yet gentle enough to protect dignity.

In My Heart ♥

When I experience Him as the Divine Mother, I feel cherished, seen, and secure: safe to be small and brave enough to begin again.

The Divine Mother looks past my dust and calls the diamond I am by name, and I rise.

From this gaze, joy wakes easily. The day feels kindly lit; colors seem warmer; even small tasks feel like care rather than duty. My voice softens, and I find myself trusting that love is the strongest teacher.

His motherly love shows me how to be tender and strong at once: to shelter without smothering, to hold and to let go. Seen this way, a kinder world appears in ordinary rooms.

In God's embrace,
my heart learns
it has always belonged.

Write your reflections here . . .

21

Sat-Chit-Ananda

God is *Sat-Chit-Ananda*: truth,
living awareness, and bliss.
This is not only His nature;
it is also a map He gives the soul.
When truth fills my awareness,
bliss naturally follows.

The Sacred Reality

God is *Sat*, the eternal Truth that never changes. He is *Chit*, the living Consciousness that awakens the sleeping soul. And God is *Ananda*, the bliss that flows when truth and awareness meet. He is constant bliss because His being is aligned with truth and awake in full consciousness.

Truth (*Sat*) by itself is beautiful, but without awareness it can remain abstract. Consciousness (*Chit*) is awareness, but without truth it can drift. When truth and consciousness are joined, truth filling awareness, the natural result is *Ananda* (bliss). This is why He is called *Sat-Chit-Ananda*. It is not only a title of praise. It is a formula for the soul's happiness.

In My Heart ♥

When I remember Him as *Sat-Chit-Ananda*, I feel He is not only showing who He is, but who I can be. Bliss is the natural fruit of living in truth and staying awake in soul-consciousness. In this, He teaches me that happiness is not fragile or dependent; it is steady, because it rests on eternal truth.

Most sorrow arises when I forget truth, when illusion, false identity, or body-consciousness colors my awareness. In such moments, even joy feels temporary. But when I return to truth, "I am a soul, God is my Parent, this cosmic play is benevolent," my awareness clears, and bliss comes back.

When I sit in remembrance of Him, truth meets awareness and something inside clicks into place, like a compass finding north. My thoughts line up, my breath smooths out, and a light, childlike ease returns: simple, spacious, free.

In God's truth and awareness,
my heart learns the secret
of unshakable bliss.

Write your reflections here . . .

22

Satyam Shivam Sundaram

God is *Satyam Shivam Sundaram*:
the Truth, the Benevolent,
the Beautiful. These are not just words
of praise; they are the path
He shows the soul.

The Sacred Reality

God is *Satyam* (truth), truth itself, unchanging, incorruptible. He is *Shivam* (benevolence), the Benefactor, whose every thought and action brings benefit to souls. And God is *Sundaram* (beauty), beautiful not in form, but in character, light, and love. His beauty is the harmony of truth and benevolence expressed perfectly.

This, too, is a formula. *Satyam* without *Shivam* can become rigid; truth without love can feel harsh. *Shivam* without *Satyam* can become blind giving, lacking clarity. But when truth and benevolence come together, *Sundaram* arises: beauty of the highest order. This is the inner radiance of a soul aligned with God.

He not only embodies *Satyam Shivam Sundaram*;
He teaches me that this is the way to live, to act with benevolence and carry goodness into relationships.
Beauty, then, is not something to decorate, but something to awaken.

In My Heart ♥

When I remember God as *Satyam Shivam Sundaram*, I realize He is not only showing who He is, but who I can become. I see that my true beauty lies in living truthfully and benevolently. This beauty cannot fade; it shines from within and grows the more I walk God's way.

In remembrance, I hear again what I had forgotten: the same beauty that lives in God lives in me; my real self is beautiful beyond description. Holding this awareness, a quiet fullness returns, and what felt closed begins to open.

And there are signs. My mind stays clean and calm. Beauty shows up as coherence: a rightness between what I know, what I say, and what I do.

In God's truth and benevolence,
my heart learns the secret
of everlasting beauty.

Write your reflections here . . .

23

The Highest and the Servant

God is the Highest on High:
the Supreme Father, the Lord of
the Three Worlds. Yet He calls Himself
the Servant of all.

The Sacred Reality

In this world, the higher one's position, the more one expects to be served. Kings demand tribute, rulers command obedience, leaders gather followers. But God's way turns this upside down. Though He is Supreme, He bows to serve.

He takes up the humblest work with the highest authority. God asks for no worship, no offerings, no recognition. Instead, He gives Shrimat, the highest directions, not as commands but as gifts. His guidance sets souls free rather than binding them to rules.

This is His paradox: the One whom no one can order chooses to obey love. His greatness shines not in being served, but in serving; not in demanding obedience, but in giving directions that lead to liberation. God's authority is expressed as service; His power manifests as humility.

In My Heart ♥

When I realize that the Highest of all has made Himself my Servant, I am both humbled and moved. Greatness is not sitting above others; it is kneeling low enough to lift them.

I receive His Shrimat with a willing heart, not because I must, but because these directions are love made practical. Keep the mind clean; give no sorrow; take no sorrow. Live with undivided loyalty to God; choose simplicity over excess. This guidance does not diminish me; it frees me to become who I truly am.

His example reshapes how I serve others. I stop trying to impress and start choosing to serve. I help restore dignity where it's been lost, ease sorrow where I can, and pass along peace and liberation as gifts received, not owned.

True leadership, I learn, is making others greater than they thought they could be.

In God's humility,
my heart learns
that real power serves.

Write your reflections here . . .

24

The Limitless in the Ordinary

Keep awareness anchored
in God, the Unlimited,
and the day's smallness cannot
narrow the heart.

The Sacred Reality

The world expects the Divine to arrive with thunder and spectacle: palaces, miracles, dazzling forms. But God reveals Himself in silence, through an ordinary human chariot, in the simplest words. His knowledge is limitless, yet He speaks as a teacher in a village schoolroom.

This is His paradox: the One who contains all wisdom makes Himself small so that we can receive Him. If God poured the full ocean into a cup, it would break. So He gives drop by drop, in ways we can grasp, through language as plain as conversation. The Unlimited hides in the limited so the limited can meet the Unlimited.

Because God comes in ordinariness, He can reach every soul. No special initiation, no elite qualification is required. God sits among the ordinary and gives extraordinary treasures. His greatness is not diminished by ordinariness; it is revealed in it.

In My Heart ♥

He tutors me in the extraordinary hidden within the ordinary. When the phone rings during dinner, I let it ring and stay present with the meal, the people I'm with. In that choice not to be pulled away, I remember: the Limitless is here. The ringing stops, and there's peace in choosing presence over urgency.

When I anchor my day in His unlimited presence, the smallest acts carry weight. Each ordinary moment becomes roomy enough for love.

At the kitchen sink, I remember He is present even in washing dishes. The task doesn't change, but my awareness does. Suddenly there's room for gratitude, for hands that can serve.

His ordinariness teaches me that greatness isn't about grand gestures; it's about bringing unlimited care to ordinary moments. I stop performing spirituality and start living it, one conscious breath at a time.

In God's ordinariness,
my heart discovers
the wonder of the Unlimited.

Write your reflections here . . .

25

The Eternal Child

God is the Supreme Father,
yet He is also the Eternal Child:
playful, tender, and light.

The Sacred Reality

In the world, children bring a unique joy. They are fresh, unburdened, and free from the calculations of adulthood. God, though the Highest, becomes the Eternal Child. He is light, approachable, and full of sweetness.

Why does the Supreme take this form? Perhaps so we can experience what the most beautiful child could be. God comes without demands, inviting love in its purest form. As the Eternal Child, He gives us the chance to create our fortune by serving Him, giving Him our attention, our time, our remembrance, as lovingly as a family would care for a cherished child.

In this paradox, the Almighty lowers Himself completely. Though God is the Ocean of Wisdom, He is innocent, like a child. Though the One holds every treasure, He lets us taste the joy of giving, and in that giving, our fortune grows beyond lifetimes. Treating Him with the tenderness we would offer a child, we learn a love that matures us.

In My Heart ♥

When I remember Him as the Eternal Child, I feel a sweetness unlike any other relationship. I delight in Him. I find myself wanting to give, not because He needs it, but because His innocence invites it.

Then playfulness arrives. I make a small seat for Him in my mind and check on Him through the day. My shoulders drop; my steps grow springy. Ordinary tasks feel like looking after someone loved. I'm quicker to laugh, quicker to begin again, and service feels like a simple, happy game.

This childlike presence teaches me that true greatness is never heavy. Walking with Him, I remain light, playful, and free.

In God's childlikeness,
my heart learns
the joy of giving with love.

Write your reflections here . . .

26

The Poet

God is the Ocean of Knowledge,
and He speaks as a Poet:
simple words that carry eternity.

The Sacred Reality

Human poets use words to stir feelings or capture fleeting beauty. God's poetry is different. His words are truth itself. He explains the essence of the scriptures in the simplest language, yet within those words lies the wisdom of eternity.

He speaks of the soul as a star, of time as a great cycle, of God as the Seed of the human tree. God paints with metaphor, not to decorate but to reveal. His language is clear, direct, even ordinary, yet the effect is extraordinary.

This is His paradox: the Unlimited chooses words that a child can grasp, yet scholars cannot exhaust.

God's poetry awakens the intellect, heals the heart, and restores the soul's dignity.

Unlike worldly poets who rely on imagination, His poetry is remembrance of reality. He brings the invisible into vision: the home of silence, the cycle of time, the inheritance of liberation. God's words are not just heard; they echo, like mantras written in the soul.

In My Heart ♥

When I listen to Him as the Poet, I feel both enlightened and moved. His images stay with me: the star, the tree, the Seed, guiding my thoughts long after the words are spoken.

God teaches me that words are not small. When used with truth and beauty, they become instruments of transformation.

Sometimes a single image shifts my day. Remembering the star quiets my mind; remembering the Seed steadies my actions. His metaphors become places I can live from, not just ideas I think about.

In difficult moments, I hold one word from Him like a lamp, and the next step appears.

In God's words,
my heart learns
that truth itself is poetry.

Write your reflections here . . .

27

The Gardener

God is the Gardener of souls,
tending each one with care, as if
it were the only plant in His garden.

The Sacred Reality

A true gardener knows that every plant is different. Some need more sunlight, others more shade. Some require pruning to grow strong, while others flourish simply by being watered gently each day. God is that Gardener for the soul.

When I connect with the Gardener, I feel His attention is exact. He knows where to place me, how much to give me, and when to hold back so I can grow. God does not treat all souls the same; He understands each one's unique nature. He never rushes, never forgets. Even when I feel withered, God does not discard me. He tends patiently until life returns.

Here is His paradox: He is the Gardener who owns nothing, yet gives everything. Worldly gardeners labor for fruit, flowers, or income and claim the harvest as their own. But God tends without self-interest. He does not keep the fruit of His garden; He offers it back to us as inheritance. His joy is not in possessing, but in watching each soul blossom.

In My Heart ♥

When I experience Him as my Gardener, I feel seen and safe. I no longer need to compare myself with others, for God knows my nature and cares for me accordingly. His patient tending gives me confidence that even in my weakest seasons, He will not abandon me.

He does not shield me from every wind; He stands with me until my roots learn to hold.

Even my mistakes become fertilizer; what once drained me slowly becomes food for new growth. And joy sprouts quietly: what was compost yesterday has turned green today.

In God's care,
my heart learns
to grow steady and whole.

Write your reflections here . . .

28

The Seed

God reveals Himself as the tiniest
form holding the greatest treasure.
He is the Seed. Tiny, subtle,
but containing everything.

The Sacred Reality

A seed looks like nothing, a dot in the hand. Yet inside it are hidden the colors of leaves, the sweetness of fruit, the shape of branches yet to come. God reveals Himself as that Seed for the whole human tree. In Him are packed the fragrance of peace, the strength of purity, the warmth of love, the sweetness of bliss, and the clarity of knowledge. He also holds within Himself the secret of time. The beginning, middle, and end of the cycle.

This is His wonder: the smallest form holds the greatest treasure. The Supreme does not need to be vast to be limitless. God concentrates eternity into a single point of light, and from that point the whole world is sustained. While the tree grows, weakens, and withers, the Seed remains unchanged. Constant, powerful, whole.

In My Heart ♥

When I discovered Him as the Seed, I stopped trying to carry the whole world in my mind. He taught me that one pure focus contains more power than scattered effort.

When my mind spins with worries, I remember God, the Seed, and feel myself drawn to what's essential. The noise falls away. Instead of trying to fix everything at once, I tend to what's essential. The root, not the branches.

This morning, facing a packed schedule, instead of multitasking everything, I remembered God as the Seed and chose one task for my full attention. That single focus carried stillness that spread to the rest of my day.

When relationships grow complicated with old hurts and expectations, I return to the seed of love that brought us together. Sometimes that return to essence cuts through years of complexity.

In God's seed-like form,
my heart learns
the power of essence.

Write your reflections here . . .

29

The Alchemist

God is the true Alchemist.
Where others see rust and ruin,
He sees hidden gold.

The Sacred Reality

In legends, alchemists were said to change iron into gold. But God is the living *Parasnath* (Alchemist), the One whose touch restores the soul. He does not work with fire or metals. God's alchemy is remembrance and love.

We souls have become covered in rust: the stains of sorrow, the corrosion of ego, the weight of time. Yet He never despairs. God knows what lies beneath. Where others see decline, He sees potential. Where others see decay, God sees the promise of renewal.

Here is the paradox: the Almighty does not force transformation. God works quietly, almost invisibly. With a glance of love and a word of truth, He dissolves what is false and draws out what is eternal. Weakness becomes strength, fear becomes courage, heaviness becomes lightness. What seemed ordinary shines again in its original brilliance.

In My Heart ♥

When I know Him as the Alchemist, hope rises in me. However dull or burdened I feel, He sees the eternal worth within. His touch assures me that the soul is never lost; it is only waiting to shine.

I bring Him my rust: regret, fatigue, old habits. Sitting in quiet remembrance, I let His gaze do the work. I offer consent instead of strain. In that willing stillness, something bright surfaces that I could not produce by effort.

I practice tiny exchanges through the day: I replace a complaint with a blessing; I replace a worry with one small step I can take. Each exchange leaves a trace of gold: first inside, then in how I see others.

In His company, self-respect returns, simple and steady. I am not pretending to be gold; I am remembering it.

In God's alchemy,
my heart learns the wonder
of becoming gold again.

Write your reflections here . . .

30

The Magician (*Jadugar*)

God is the Magician of truth,
the *Jadugar* who creates wonder
without illusion.

The Sacred Reality

Worldly magicians work with tricks and smoke, distracting the eye while hiding the hand. Their magic is clever, but it fades when the show is over. God's magic is different. His wonder is real. With no disguise, no sleight of hand, He changes the soul itself.

He takes what is broken and makes it whole. God turns a beggar into a king, sorrow into joy, confusion into clarity. And He does it not with drama but with a glance of love and a few simple words. God's magic does not deceive; it reveals. What seemed impossible becomes natural when He is near.

Here is the paradox: the most astonishing Magician does not perform in public. His magic is quiet, almost hidden. The world rushes after spectacle, but His wonders happen in silence. The Highest *Jadugar* creates the greatest show without ever stepping onto a stage.

In My Heart ♥

When I experience Him as the Magician, the air inside me changes. Quiet brightens. I have not moved, yet a room opens within.

A knot I wrestled with for years loosens on its own. A door I kept pushing suddenly swings from the other side. The heavy thing becomes light.

I place a small trouble in His palm and watch it turn: fear becomes courage, irritation becomes goodwill, hurry becomes breath. What I called "impossible" becomes simple; the "me" I thought I was, my labels, was just dust covering the mirror.

I find myself smiling for no reason. His magic doesn't carry me away from life; it returns me to it: clear, kind, awake. I walk out lighter, as if Someone quietly gave me back to myself.

In God's magic,
my heart learns the wonder
of being made new.

Write your reflections here . . .

31

The All-Embracing One

God is the All-Embracing One,
the Supreme who holds every soul
close without distinction.

The Sacred Reality

The world divides and excludes. Human love narrows to "my people, my family, my nation." But God's love is limitless. He does not embrace one and reject another. God does not look at race, nationality, gender, or history. For Him, every soul is a child: equally precious, equally beloved.

Here is the paradox: the One who is beyond attachment is also the One who embraces most fully. God's love is not limited by need or demand. He is detached, yet never distant. God holds all but clings to none. God's love is as wide as the sky, yet as intimate as a whisper inside the heart.

In My Heart ♥

When I experience Him as the All-Embracing One, loneliness loosens its grip. In the quiet before dawn or the noise of noon, I feel nurtured and I belong, not because I have earned it, but because I am. Under that gaze, the part of me that calls itself "rejected" falls silent: I am cherished.

His embrace is not of arms but of vision. He looks without flinching at what I try to hide: the envy I disguise, the sharp word I regret. He holds me within my original beauty, my eternal dignity.

Being seen like this gives me courage to see myself through His eyes. I sit with what aches until it softens; I name what is tangled without fear. In that light, shame loses its teeth; what felt unlovable becomes held, and what was fractured begins to line up again.

From this inner wholeness, I find myself giving blessings more easily: to the person who cuts in line, to the friend whose problems always seem more important, to the person who always needs to be right. Not because they deserve it, but because God's all-embracing love overflows through me.

In God's embrace,
being seen becomes being healed.

Write your reflections here . . .

32

The Teacher

God is the Teacher, the One who teaches not from books, but from truth itself.

The Sacred Reality

Worldly teachers speak to personalities. They address the title I carry, the body I inhabit. Their words reach the surface, but rarely the essence. God speaks to me as I truly am: a soul. His words bypass the mask and awaken the dignity that lies hidden within.

Worldly teachers also pass on what they themselves have learned. Their knowledge is borrowed, gathered from books or tradition. God is different. He says, "I have knowledge, but I have not studied with anyone." God is the Teacher who teaches without ever having been taught.

And God's syllabus is simple: "Consider yourself a soul and remember Me."

Here is the paradox: the Supreme Teacher uses the simplest words, yet they contain the wisdom of eternity and prepare His children for kingship.

In My Heart ♥

When I know Him as my Teacher, He becomes the primary relationship of my day. He addresses the soul with clarity and precision.

In a world where even loving parents entrust their children's education to others, I marvel that the Highest on High sits with me personally, making Himself available to teach this one small heart.

He gives me "homework" that actually works: begin and end the day in quiet remembrance; pause each hour for a minute of soul-awareness. Discipline feels like care, and consistency becomes love in action.

He teaches me how to earn an eternal income, not money, but an unstealable fortune.

The Supreme Teacher prepares me for the real exam: life itself. The tests arrive as situations, and He whispers the open-book hint: remember who you are; remember the One.

Under His teaching, I learn to teach by remaining a student, quietly passing on what He has made real in me.

In God's teaching,
I gather a wealth of peace,
power, and love that cannot be lost.

Write your reflections here . . .

33

The Supreme Father

God is the Supreme Father,
the One who gives love and a vision greater
than I could imagine.

The Sacred Reality

Earthly fathers do their best to protect and guide, but their vision is limited to this life, this time. The Supreme Father is different. His love is unlimited, and He also gives perspective. He speaks of the destiny of His children as rulers of a golden age. God says: "I am your Father. Belong to Me and I will make you the masters of *Satyug*."

God comes to lift my eyes beyond the small struggles of today. He reveals where the world has come from and what role I play in the eternal story. God's care is intimate, but His vision is magnificent. He restores not just my peace, but my future.

The paradox is this: the Highest on High, the Lord of the Three Worlds, chooses to sit with me as a Father, not a distant king. He explains and bestows the inheritance of the soul.

In My Heart ♥

When I know Him as the Supreme Father, I hear a quiet certainty: "You are Mine." Something in me stops wandering. I am no longer defined by my past; I belong by right of relationship.

He gives me keys to the house: the trust of self-sovereignty. God teaches the family way: keep truth clean, carry yourself with dignity. This is a standard to rise to because His name is on me.

He trains me for an inheritance: steadiness under praise and blame, generosity even in lack. These are the signs of royalty being born.

I am not a self-made soul; I am a well-fathered one. His hopes in me become my rightful hope for myself, and my steps start to match His vision.

*In His fatherhood,
my heart learns
the responsibility
of a rightful heir.*

Write your reflections here . . .

34

The True Guide (*Satguru*)

God is the *Satguru*, the only
Guide who leads souls Home.

The Sacred Reality

There are many gurus in the world, but their guidance is limited. They may offer practices, rituals, or words of comfort, yet their reach does not extend beyond the body or this short life. Their advice often reflects their own learning or opinion. God is different.

As *Satguru*, God's guidance is unlimited. He does not show me a temporary path, but the way back to my eternal Home. His *Shrimat*, His elevated directions, is not based on opinion but on truth. God's guidance is filled with fortune.

Here is the paradox: God's directions are firm, yet they bring freedom. By following Him, I do not lose myself; I find myself.

In My Heart ❤

When I know Him as *Satguru*, the noise in me quiets. I no longer need ten opinions; I need His one direction. With a minute of stillness, I ask, "Is this *Shrimat* or my habit?" and the next step becomes clear.

He does not hand me the whole map; He gives me the next true turn. I take that step, and help meets me on the road. Doors open that I could not push. This is how I learn trust: not by seeing everything, but by walking with the One who does.

I trade cleverness for obedience, speed for accuracy, guilt for clean starts. If I miss a turn, I stop and realign.

I notice the signs He taught me to watch for: peace without passivity, courage without aggression, simplicity without loss. Where *Shrimat* leads, dignity grows. Where I follow, fortune follows.

The path Home is not far away;
it begins the moment I listen
and take one faithful step.

Write your reflections here . . .

35

The Eternal Beloved

God is the Eternal Beloved,
the One my heart has been searching
for across lifetimes.

The Sacred Reality

All the world's love stories are faint echoes of this one truth: there is only One Beloved who never leaves. Human love thrills, then fades. People change, promises break, bodies perish. But God's love is constant: pure, tender, limitless. He whispers through time, "You are Mine, and I am yours."

When I turn to Him, I feel seen as I never have before: no mask, no pretense, no fear of rejection. God sees the beauty I had forgotten and delights in it.

Here is the wonder: God is the Highest on High, yet He chooses to be my Beloved. He has no need, yet He offers Himself. God is beyond attachment, yet He gives me the deepest experience of belonging. Because no one is higher than He is, the One never becomes attracted in the human sense; His love is pure, free from the neediness that marks human affection.

In My Heart ♥

When I experience Him as my Beloved, the restless ache ends.

What I longed for in worldly love: to be fully seen and chosen without audition; to be safe, kept, and never left; to be understood and delighted in; to be told the truth gently; to be remembered and wanted for my highest, arrives all at once.

God is constancy without possession, intimacy without fear, a truthful mirror that doesn't wound, a sanctuary that doesn't close.

With Him I am known, enjoyed, and made truer; my secrets rest, my courage returns, my joy becomes playful again. The "soul mate" I sought was the One who meets me, soul to Supreme Soul, and frees me to love without grasping, to belong without losing myself.

In God's love,
my heart learns
what it means
to be cherished forever.

Write your reflections here . . .

36

The Bestower of Blessings (*Vardata*)

God is the Bestower of Blessings. His blessings come from the heart, not just the lips, and they touch every thought, every word, every action.

The Sacred Reality

In the world, those who give do so sparingly. They weigh what they offer, expecting gratitude or return. Even generous hearts eventually grow tired. As the *Vardata*, God says, "The Bestower of Blessings Himself becomes yours."

His blessings are not mere words; they are currents of strength, peace, and fortune. God's blessings aren't earned; they're received through alignment. His vision itself is a blessing: He looks at me with faith, seeing the best in me until I learn to see it myself.

Here is the paradox: God is the richest of all, yet He keeps nothing for Himself. He gives endlessly, yet His treasures do not diminish. The more God gives, the more I realize He was never giving things, but awakening what was already mine.

In My Heart ♥

When I belong to the Bestower of Blessings Himself, what could be missing? It feels as if the seed is in my hand: one honest moment of remembering, and what seemed far comes near.

His blessings arrive as goodwill, pure feeling, and real hope. He calls me fortunate and capable. Holding that truth, something in me begins again.

He is easy to please: He loves the word One: strength from One, remembrance of One. When I keep my promise simple, one steady loyalty, one quiet yes, the way opens.

Blessings grow by giving. I pass them on in quiet ways: a pure intention, a small kindness, and the current strengthens.

Gratitude becomes my posture, not a performance. I thank Him first and find I'm already standing in yesterday's blessings.

In God's blessings,
my heart learns that generosity
is the natural language of love.

Write your reflections here . . .

37

The Spiritual Flame (*Ruhani Shama*)

God is the *Ruhani Shama*,
the eternal Flame that lights every
soul without ever diminishing.

The Sacred Reality

In the world, flames flicker and fade. A candle burns down, a fire consumes itself. The Supreme Flame is different. God shines without fuel, without loss. His light is spiritual: the light of truth, love, and purity that never goes out.

When He comes, He ignites what has grown dim. Souls, covered by the ashes of sorrow and forgetfulness, catch light again in God's presence. Just as one flame can light a thousand lamps without weakening, He kindles every soul and yet remains full. God's radiance awakens and purifies.

Here is the paradox: the tiniest point of light is also the brightest flame of all. God is subtle, yet His light reaches everywhere. He is incorporeal, yet He burns away the heaviest darkness. God's fire does not destroy; it restores.

In My Heart ♥

When I experience Him as the *Ruhani Shama*, I feel my inner lamp catch again. He doesn't tell me to shine; one touch, and I remember I am light too.

The Spiritual Flame teaches me how to tend the flame. I pour the oil of remembrance often, not just in crisis. I set a clear glass of honesty around the flame so the winds of opinion can't blow it out. Then I lift the lamp higher, not to be seen, but to help others see.

In quiet moments I return to the point of light, and rays of peace begin to move through me: first as calm, then as clarity, and finally as deep silence.

I no longer chase brightness; I stay near the Source. What once felt heavy loses its shadow. What seemed complicated becomes plain on a lit path.

In God's flame,
my heart becomes a lighthouse
in any storm.

Write your reflections here . . .

38

The Unshakeable One

God is the Unshakeable One:
perfectly still in a world that startles.

The Sacred Reality

Around us, life jerks and jolts. News breaks, tempers flare, alarms sound; minds rush to react. God is different. His stillness is not distance or indifference; it is the strength of complete inner alignment. Nothing outside can enter to disturb what is whole within. God's peace runs ocean-deep; His quiet carries more truth than any outcry; His patience rests on a center that does not move.

This stillness is alive. God is not asleep to the world; He is most awake: aware of all, attached to none, clear, measured, serene. From this clarity, God acts without agitation and speaks without haste. Where noise confuses, His silence steadies.

Here is the paradox: the One who is most aware is least disturbed. Perfect consciousness creates perfect stillness.

In My Heart ♥

When I remember Him as the Unshakeable One, reactivity loosens. The urge to defend, explain, or control quiets, and I come back to God, the luminous One.

The Unshakeable One teaches me simple anchors. I take one slow breath, affirm "I am a soul," and place a gentle full stop. I ask, "Is this mine to carry?"

I practice soft strength: heart soft, presence gentle. I hold peace like a lamp, not a wall. I let a little silence finish my sentence. I choose response over reaction, accuracy over speed.

When pressure rises, anger heats, fear hurries, I borrow His pace. I allow time to be my ally. I do what is mine and leave the rest with the One who cannot be provoked.

Storms still come; waves still rise. Standing where He stands, I notice that what shook me yesterday barely moves me today. Steadiness becomes natural, and freedom follows.

In God's stillness,
my heart learns a strength
that nothing can shake.

Write your reflections here . . .

39

Trikaldarshi (Seer of the Three Aspects of Time)

God is *Trikaldarshi*,
the One who sees past, present,
and future with perfect clarity.

The Sacred Reality

Human vision is short. We see what is near and stumble at what is far. Memory distorts the past, emotion clouds the present, and fear blinds the future. But God is different. As *Trikaldarshi*, He holds all three aspects of time in one gaze. He knows the story of the beginning, middle, and end. Nothing is hidden; nothing is uncertain.

This is why God's guidance carries such weight. When He speaks, He is not guessing or predicting; God is revealing what already is: the truth of the cycle of time, the destiny of souls, the return of a golden age.

Here is the paradox: the vastness of the cycle is held in His mind, yet He leans close to guide a single step of mine. God knows the destiny of the world, yet He cares for the details of my journey.

In My Heart ♥

When I remember Him as *Trikaldarshi*, my mind stops arguing with time. I sit in His steady gaze and become a detached observer; the rush to fix the past or control the future loses its force. Peace returns, and with it, accuracy.

I bless what has been and let it be finished. I live by signal, not panic. If the way is clear, I move; if it is not, I keep still without fear. Delay becomes protection; a closed door becomes direction. He holds the sequence; I keep the sincerity.

When I miss it, I realign quickly: no self-accusation, just check and change. Wasteful thoughts dissolve in remembrance of Him; strength gathers in silence; courage returns in service.

In God's vision,
my heart releases what was,
does what is right,
and lets what will be arrive on time.

Write your reflections here . . .

40

The All-Powerful One (*Sarva Shaktiman*)

God is the All-Powerful One,
and by remembering Him,
we receive soul-power.

The Sacred Reality

In the world, power wears countless masks: wealth commanding resources, technology reshaping behavior, position directing nations, knowledge unlocking mysteries. Yet earthly power is often corrupted by its own weight. Authority hardens into arrogance; strength calcifies into domination.

Divine power is different. He declares, "I am *Sarva Shaktiman* because My soul is ever-pure." Here lies the secret: true power springs from absolute purity. His might restores, removing the alloy of vice and revealing the soul's hidden gold. His strength works quietly, subtly.

Consider the paradox: the Supreme Authority operates without ego. The One who could command worlds chooses to serve.

In My Heart ♥

When I discovered Him as *Sarva Shaktiman*, the meaning of strength changed. The world taught me power meant control; He shows me it is connection.

He whispers, "You are My child, a junior *Sarva Shaktiman* from birth," not earned by struggle, but inherited by love. The moment I belong to Him, I belong to His strength.

I see how my soul's battery dimmed from running on my own small generators of will and want. In remembrance, restoration begins: the stone intellect softens like ice touched by spring.

Now, when I turn to the Pure One, real power returns. It is the courage to give and give again, to place a full stop on runaway thoughts, to love generously, to discern quietly, and to face my own insecurities without flinching.

True authority begins within: mastery of thought, victory over vice, sovereignty of conscience. This is the strength that endures, a kingship expressed as truthfulness, compassion, and self-respect. It does not conquer people; it frees the soul.

In God's all-powerful nearness,
my heart receives the strength
to be pure, peaceful, and free.

Begin here each day
to let peace become
your atmosphere.

APPENDIX: DAILY DIVINE CONNECTION

Begin each day by opening to any chapter in *Experiencing God*. Choose one sentence from either section that speaks to your heart today.

Take three deep breaths. Inhale slowly, pause, then exhale completely. Let this rhythm center you in the present moment.

Release distractions and open your heart to divine connection. You might sense this as radiant light approaching, or simply rest in quiet awareness. However it appears to you, welcome this presence with an open heart. Let your chosen words resonate deep within, settling like a gentle friend.

Experience this as God's embrace. Personal, loving, present.

Receive this connection fully. Allow divine presence to nourish your spirit and fill you with peace.

Trust that in this moment, all is well. Let this sacred awareness take root within you.

The noise of daily concerns fades, leaving only His presence and tranquility. God's nearness brings peace and clarity to your mind. You feel renewed purpose. The world appears brighter.

Your steps feel light, supported by divine grace. With each moment, awareness of God's presence grows stronger. These moments of stillness give you strength for life's journey.

Carry this one sentence with you through your day, returning to it whenever you need peace.

Om Shanti.

ACKNOWLEDGMENTS

I've been blessed with many guides along this spiritual path: teachers, friends, and fellow travelers who offered light when I needed it most. I carry deep gratitude for each one.

But the true source and sustainer of this book is God. Of all the people He could have chosen as His instrument, He graciously entrusted this work to me. I am humbled, honored, and deeply grateful.

Writing this book was different from anything I've ever experienced. Each time I sat down to begin a chapter, I felt myself drawn into a sacred space where words seemed to flow effortlessly, as if they were being given to me directly. What could have been difficult work became pure joy; what might have felt burdensome was surprisingly light. It was a gift to receive and a joy to offer back.

All credit belongs to Him. To me belongs only the happiness of returning what He gave.

Offered to the One from whom all pure love flows.

ABOUT THE AUTHOR

I'm Shireen Chada. For over three decades and more than 20,000 hours of practice, I've walked the path from seeking to knowing. I've studied with the **Brahma Kumaris** and discovered how meditation becomes not just something you do, but who you are.

My work is simple: I help you remember who you truly are and come home to yourself. I've written books like ***Awakening from the Matrix***, ***Oh My Goodness!***, and ***Soul Fitness***. You can find my guided meditations on **Insight Timer** and the **Release Your Wings** YouTube channel, and I co-host the **Spiritual Sense** podcast.

Whether you're navigating change, longing for stillness, or searching for deeper meaning, these offerings are meant to be a gentle hand on your shoulder, guiding you back to peace and presence.

My meditations weave together sacred wisdom with the kind of soul-deep stillness that changes everything. If you take nothing else from our time together, let it be this: you are deeply loved and divinely guided.

Wherever you go,
your peace is your presence.
Your stillness is a gift,
your remembrance a light,
and your life a quiet blessing
to the world.

Om Shanti.

www.ingramcontent.com/pod-product-compliance
Lightning Source LLC
Chambersburg PA
CBHW061547250926
52052CB00010B/3107
* 9 7 8 1 9 4 1 8 8 3 2 0 4 *